Spells

for

Success

Spells for Success

Antonia Beattie

BARNES
&NOBLE
BOOKS
NEW YORK

Contents

Success Spells

* ⭐ *

The Success of Spells

The sense of success is a heady feeling, exhilarating and triumphant. Everything seems easier, and your confidence can skyrocket. Spellcraft is well-suited to helping you find the success you desire. The spells in this book have been developed with the aim of making sure that in many of the areas in which you would like to succeed, you will be fruitful.

Many traditional good luck spells have been used over the centuries to attract Lady Luck, especially when things do not look terribly rosy. Charms, such as saying words three times, talismans, and amulets, such as a mounted rabbit's foot, have many traditional associations with success.

This book gives you a number of good luck spells to use for most of your endeavors, both at home and in your work.

In this book, there are also spells for achieving your personal goals, gaining popularity, and helping you follow your dream. Spells for financial success are provided, along with spells for that much sought-after promotion, an important job interview, or even finishing a complicated project at work.

This book also contains spells that help guard you against loss of money or loss of respect, and provide protection against the envy that success can generate in others.

We hope that the spells in this book will help you find success, contentment and happiness within your own heart and the hearts of your loved ones.

Simple Spellcraft

Spellcraft is safe and effective and can be done by anyone. Spells are also an excellent way to focus your mind on how you wish to succeed.

Before casting a spell for success in a particular venture, do the following three things:

1 Clear your mind of any feelings of being unworthy of success. These generalized feelings of unworthiness plague all of us sometimes. Do not let these feelings get in the way of your spellcraft. One useful exercise is to imagine these feelings being compressed so that they fit on the head of a pin. Light a candle and pass the pin quickly over the flame. Imagine that the smoke from this flame carries away all your feelings of unworthiness – these feelings are now as unsubstantial as a few wisps of smoke.

2 Have a bath or shower to clear your mind of your everyday worries and anxieties. Wash yourself thoroughly, imagining that you are also washing away the mental and psychic grime of the day. If you don't have much time, simply wash your

hands and visualize the soap also washing away
your cares. However, for an important spell, it
is always advisable to wash your whole body
thoroughly beforehand.

3 Prepare your room or special space before
casting your spell, gathering all the necessary
tools and ingredients. If you are feeling troubled or
under siege, imagine a line of blue light running
around you protecting you from your fears and
outside distractions.

You are now ready to do some spellcraft.

Spell Tips

ne of the most important parts of spellcraft is to work out what you truly want the spell to achieve. Do you really want lots of money, or do you actually want something that the money could buy, such as a new house? This book has a number of spells, covering success in many areas – gaining popularity, finding financial success or being a successful applicant for a coveted job.

Once you have worked out what you want and you find a spell in this book that you would like to do, follow our instructions carefully for best results. If you feel that you would like to do the spell in another way, write your spell in a book especially set aside for recording your spells, then monitor the outcome of the spell after it has been cast.

Another important aspect of spellcasting is to be mindful of all the ingredients and all the actions required to cast the spell. Keep your mind focused on everything you are doing and take time to use all your senses to appreciate the power of each individual ingredient in the spell. Imbue your tools with a sense of power and purpose by briefly holding them while saying:

> *"I commit this [insert name of tool here] to [insert the purpose of the spell]."*

At all times during the preparation and casting of the spell, feel the energy of the earth. This can be done by standing on the ground with bare feet and consciously visualizing a flow of energy through your feet from the ground. Imagine that this energy is flowing through your body, looping at the top of your head, then flowing back through your body to the ground.

Personal Success

Attracting Personal Success

What do I need?

A gold metallic pen

A round copper disk

A small bag made from gold fabric, large enough to contain the disk

*T*his is a general spell to help you tap into your personal power. The main symbol that you will use in this spell is a rune that is symbolic of balanced spiritual and worldly power.

Runes have been used for centuries in magic work. The runes developed as letters of the ancient Germanic languages, and also as symbols of the various mysteries of life.

What should I do?

Gather your tools and stand where you can see or feel the rays of the sun. As you stand, become conscious of your feet and the energy of the earth under them. Imagine the energy rising through your body.

As the energy travels through your chest, raise your arms (with your tools in your hands) and stretch your body up towards the sun. Keep your feet firmly planted on the ground.

When you feel energized by the earth and sun, drop your hands and draw the rune on the copper disk. Write your full name on the reverse of the disk.

Place the disk into its golden bag and hang the bag over a spot in your home where you spend a lot of time, such as your bed.

When should I do this spell?

At noon during the phase of the new moon

Finding Success for a Personal Goal

What do I need?

A white- or natural-colored candle and a stable candle holder

A clock

A faceted lead crystal on a chain or plastic-coated string

Do you want to lose weight? Have you ever wanted to learn a new language? You may have a number of personal goals that you have trouble accomplishing because there is too much pressure to finish work commitments first. This tends to leave too little time to make commitments for yourself. Try the following general spell to help you find success for your special personal goal.

What should I do?

Sit at a table other than your work desk. Light the candle and place it in front of you so that you can look comfortably at the flame. Place the clock behind the candle.

Concentrate on the candle flame. Visualize the energy of the earth traveling up the candle into the wick, and imagine that the candle flame is then releasing this energy into the world.

Hold the faceted lead crystal over the flame and imagine that the energy is being diverted towards the clock.

Say the following words:

*"I shall succeed in [insert personal goal here].
I am directing this energy toward having the time
to complete my goal successfully.
So it shall be."*

When you are ready, extinguish the flame. Keep the candle near the clock until you achieve success with this goal.

When should I do this spell?

During the phase of the new moon

Finding Your True Beauty

What do I need?

A bunch of fresh fennel

A clear quartz crystal

True, long-lasting success often comes from self-awareness – a deep knowledge of your own true worth. Try this spell for finding your true beauty whenever you feel down or have had a rough day. This spell can also be used before going to a job interview, or asking for a pay rise or promotion. The herb used in this spell is fennel, which is renowned for its ability to protect against negative energies and aid meditation.

What should I do?

Form the fennel into a closely-packed nest onto which you can set your clear quartz crystal. Clear quartz crystals are extremely useful in spellcasting, as they can store your thoughts or the intentions of your spell.

Sit in a comfortable position with the fennel-and-crystal nest in front of you. Smell the fresh fennel and concentrate on the clear crystal. Visualize the crystal energized with pure joy. Look at the crystal and imagine what pure joy would feel like.

When you feel ready, pick up the crystal and imagine the stone literally throbbing with the energy of pure joy. Hold the crystal and let its energy surround you. Now think about who you are. Use only positive and loving terms. Recognize that you are a good and truly beautiful person.

When you are ready, take three deep breaths and place the crystal back on its nest of fennel. Carry this crystal with you when you have had a difficult day or when you feel the need for extra support.

When should I do this spell?

Any time

Gaining Popularity

What do I need?

Mint chewing gum

Two round copper disks

A black marker pen

A gold- or yellow-colored envelope

here are a great many popularity spells, some using magnets, others using special talismans. We have devised a simple spell that uses the most straightforward symbolism to increase your popularity to help you attract new friends. You may vary the spell by focusing on attracting friends who are influential or mentors to help you in your work.

What should I do?

Pop the chewing gum in your mouth and chew for a few minutes, savoring the mint flavor. Mint is often used in spellcraft to attract success to a spell or venture.

As you are chewing, write your name on one side of one copper disk with the black marker pen. On the other disk, write the word "friends" or "mentors."

When the gum is sticky, place it between the two copper disks, making a chewing gum sandwich. Make sure the words are facing the chewing gum.

Take the gold or yellow envelope, and under the flap write the words "I am popular." Place the copper disks inside the envelope. Seal the envelope and place it near your front door or near the entrance to your room.

When should I do this spell?

During the phase of the new moon

Following Your Dream

What do I need?

A bay leaf

A black marker pen with a fine point

Gold fabric made into a bag large enough to contain the bay leaf and the chosen herbs. You may wish to decorate the bag with a fringe.

Needle and thread in a color that matches the bag

Often the first step to following your dream is to know what your true dream is. A true dream is one that is yours alone, not part of the expectations of those around you. The following spell involves making a dream pillow containing herbs that will help you relax and allow your subconscious to capture your true dream and to find the best path toward successfully fulfilling your goals in life.

What should I do?

Write the following words on the bay leaf with your black marker pen:

"I follow my dream."

Place the bay leaf inside the fabric bag and fill the bag with your herb or herbs. Neatly sew the bag

20

shut, using thread that matches the fabric.

Keep the bag under your pillow for three nights. Keep a journal beside your bed and write down the dreams you can remember when you wake up. Review your journal and see if there are any useful tips on helping you find and follow your dream in life.

also ...

One or more of the following dried or fresh herbs (enough to fill your bag):

Anise

Agrimony

Hop

Lavender

Mugwort

Peppermint

Your journal

When should I do this spell?

During the phase of the full moon

Success at Work

Attracting Employment

What do I need?

A flat piece of cedarwood (approximately 2 ½ inches or 6 cm square or round)

A fine-point silver marker pen

Red cloth made from natural fibers

This spell is designed to attract employment that suits you, as opposed to just any job. The focus of this spell is on the making of a special talisman. A talisman is an object with magical powers directed to a specific purpose.

There are many types of talisman, including those that tap into the power of the planets. To encourage employment and disperse a sense of apathy and boredom, we have chosen a talisman that vibrates to the planet Mars for this spell.

What should I do?

On the wood, use your silver marker pen to draw the grid on the next page. Draw a draft grid first on a piece of paper to make sure you have the grid dimensions correct.

11	24	7	20	3
4	12	25	8	16
17	5	13	21	9
10	18	1	14	22
23	6	19	2	15

When should
I do this
spell?

On a Tuesday

If you have difficulties drawing the Mars square
onto your wood, try photocopying and pasting it
onto the wood, using your silver marker to reinforce
the lines. Wrap the talisman in the red cloth and
keep it with you at all times until you get a job.

Success at a Job Interview

What do I need?

A clean soft cloth

A sprig of fresh rosemary

A black tassel

Feng shui has a number of useful techniques to help you succeed at a job interview. We are going to weave Eastern and Western mysteries together to give you a spell that will help you to succeed. To enhance the flow of beneficial energy to you during your interview, make sure that your back is not facing the door of the interview room. Even if the chair is positioned for you to sit there, make sure that you move it so that you can see the doorway.

What should I do?

There are several stages to this spell. On the morning of your interview, clear all the money, papers and other items out of your wallet, purse, briefcase or handbag. Take your cloth and clean out any accumulated lint and dust. This is symbolic of clearing out old negative energy.

Put back only the most necessary items, making sure that everything is neat and tidy. Put the sprig of rosemary in your briefcase or handbag and tie the black tassel to the handle. If you don't want the tassel to show, carry it in your pocket.

Rosemary is an excellent herb to protect you from a negative response to your application. It is also useful for stimulating your memory, helping you remember your preparations for the interview.

Tassels are used to disperse negative energy, and the color black symbolizes strength and perseverance.

When should I do this spell?

Sometime before your appointment on the day of the interview

Getting Recognition

A strip of parchment-style paper about 6 inches (15 cm) long and 2 inches (5 cm) wide

A red pen

A red ribbon long enough to tie the piece of paper when it is rolled up

A sprig of rosemary

There are times when you just can't seem to get the recognition that you deserve.

Sometimes people who do their work well find themselves being taken for granted. To attract recognition and acknowledgment try the following spell. This spell features a name charm, which can be used to subtly heighten the awareness of your name in the workplace.

What should I do?

On a break during work, use the red pen to write your name repeatedly on the strip of paper until one side is covered with your name.

Roll up the piece of paper and tie it with the length of red ribbon. Break off a short stem of rosemary and tuck it between the ribbon and the paper.

If you work at a desk, place the rolled paper so that it sits right in front of you, at the top of your desk. If this area of your desk is cluttered, tidy it immediately. In feng shui, this section of your desk corresponds with fame and acknowledgment.

When should I do this spell?

During the phase of the new moon

Getting a Promotion

What do I need?

A pinch of the following:

Coriander powder

Cumin powder

Curry powder

Black cracked pepper

Ground tarragon

Tobacco

Caraway seeds

Ground coffee

*I*n busy organizations, promotions are sometimes overlooked, as everyone feels stressed in trying to meet deadlines or budget. Being overlooked does not necessarily indicate that your workplace does not value you – promotions or pay raises may just be at the bottom of the "To-Do" list.

Try the following spell to tap into the planetary powers of Mars and Mercury if you want extra support in asking for a promotion.

What should I do?

Place all the ingredients in the jar, measuring out the dried ingredients first, then pouring in the aloe vera juice. It is best if the aloe vera juice has been freshly collected that morning from the fleshy leaves of the plant.

With the metal spoon, stir the ingredients together while visualizing yourself in the process of asking for a promotion. Imagine feeling strong and in control. When ready, screw the lid onto the jar and take it to work with you.

Aloe vera and the color of amber correspond with success, while the herbs are a mixture of plants that correspond to Mars and Mercury. Mars will give you a sense of courage, and Mercury will give you the eloquence to state your case.

also ...

Three tablespoons of juice from an aloe vera plant

An amber-colored glass jar with a secure screw-on lid

A small metal spoon

When should I do this spell?

About 8 am on a Tuesday or a Wednesday

Finishing a Complicated Project

What do I need?

A black cardboard square measuring 1 ½ inches (4 cm) square

A silver fine-point marker pen

Your files, papers, models, plans or another physical manifestation of your project

Your journal

A complicated, involved project can seem as if it is never going to end. There is often a certain point just before everything is finalized when you feel as if the project is going to collapse or that you will never make the deadline.

Try the following spell to help you steer the project to completion. You will be making a talisman that corresponds with the planetary energy of Saturn, the planet renowned for inspiring discipline to achieve goals.

What should I do?

On the black cardboard, draw the following grid with your silver marker pen:

4	9	2
3	5	7
8	1	6

On the reverse of the cardboard, draw the following symbol for Saturn:

Place the square talisman on the files, stack of papers, plan, model or other manifestation of your project or, if you are having trouble thinking through the final stages of the project, place the talisman under your pillow for three nights.

Keep a journal near you, and record the dreams you can remember on awakening. Your dreams may give you the solution to the final stages of the project. You may also find that you wake up with the energy or determination to complete the project.

When should I do this spell?

About 3 pm on a Saturday afternoon

Getting Picked to Do a Job

A wooden disk measuring 2 ½ inches (5 cm) in diameter

A black marker pen

A picture of an eye (perhaps from a picture of one of your favorite people)

A gold marker pen

If a special project that is of interest to you or that could ultimately lead to further recognition or a promotion crops up in your workplace, or if you are submitting a tender or wooing a prestigious client, the following spell will help you stand out from the pack.

The spell involves making a success amulet that can be worn next to your skin when you are working on your proposal and during business meetings.

What should I do?

With your black marker pen, mark the center of the disk with a dot. Draw two lines through the center, perpendicular to each other, making an equal arm cross.

In the middle of the disk, paste the symbol of the eye. The eye wards off negative vibrations that may badly affect your chances of getting the job.

In each quadrant of the disk, write one of the following words:

Courage
Eloquence
Wisdom
Persistence

Around the edge of the disk, draw a circle of gold with your gold pen. Carry this disk with you until you are successful in getting the job.

When should I do this spell?

When you first start working toward getting the job

Financial Success

What do I need?

A piece of paper that is, or looks like, parchment, sized to fit comfortably in the bag when rolled up

A green pen

A length of thin green ribbon

A bag made from green silk or linen

A gold-colored coin

Attracting Good Fortune

There are a number of charms, amulets and talismans that help attract good fortune. This spell focuses on making an ancient amulet to realign the energies around you, allowing you to receive the good fortune you wish to attract. Wear it whenever you are using your money, for example, when you are shopping or doing your accounts.

What should I do?

Collect your ingredients and tools. Write your full name on the piece of parchment with the green pen. Roll up the parchment and tie it with the green ribbon. Place this and the gold-colored coin in the bag.

Take your needle and thread and sew around the top edge of the bag to close it. Pull the thread so that the fabric bunches up. Sew a few more stitches to secure the gathered fabric.

With the same thread, if possible, make a loop big enough to thread your leather thong through. The ends of the thong can be simply tied into a knot at the desired length.

also ...

Needle and thread

A leather thong, long enough to allow the amulet to hang close to your heart

When should I do this spell?

On a Thursday at 10 pm

Attracting Money for a Particular Purpose

What do I need?

A picture of what you want to buy

A stable wooden candle holder

A green candle

Matches

Candle magic is a powerful way of getting what you want. The green-colored candle corresponds with the earth element and the related concepts of growth and nurture. Money spells usually feature a lot of green symbols.

The following spell also features a picture, which is usually placed underneath the candle holder to direct the energy specifically to what you want to buy. Although the picture is only representative of your wish, try to find an image that includes as many details of your wish as possible. You may even wish to draw the image.

What should I do?

Find a safe place in your room where you can leave your candle to burn without damaging anything. Put the picture on a stable, non-flammable surface, then put the wooden candle holder on top of it, so that an edge of the picture is still visible.

Place the candle in the holder. Light the candle. Sit comfortably and concentrate on your breathing, breathing in for a count of four and breathing out for a count of four, while staring into the flame.

When you feel ready, close your eyes and visualize what you want. Construct the image in your mind in every detail, seeing it in the position of your "third eye" (in the middle of your forehead).

When you feel that you have created a strong enough mental image, anchor the spell to the picture by touching it. Leave the candle to burn down to the end, keeping the picture beneath the candle holder.

When should I do this spell?

On a Thursday at 10 pm

Investing Money Wisely

What do I need?

A copy of a statement of your investment account from when it had the largest amount of money from a successful investment, or a blank piece of paper

A crystal pendulum hanging from a chain

A notebook

Time, information, and expertise are needed to ensure that you make the right investment decisions and do not fall prey to "get-rich-quick" schemes. However, you also need a bit of luck. This spell is designed to help you tap into a form of universal intelligence that will help you decide when to invest and whose advice to heed.

What should I do?

Take a photocopy or printout of your investment statement. This sets up a history of success.

If you do not have an investment portfolio yet, write on the piece of paper the amount of money that you want to get as a return for your investment.

Hold the chain of the pendulum between your thumb and forefinger. If you are not familiar with pendulums, play with it for a while, asking it which way is "yes" and which way is "no." Record its movements in the notebook.

When you are ready, place your elbow on a table so that you can comfortably hang the pendulum over the statement or piece of paper. Now ask your question, such as:

> *"Shall I invest [insert amount] in this project?"*
> *"Shall I follow [insert name]'s advice?"*

Keep a record of the pendulum's responses and the fate of the investment. You may wish to try this method on small investments before using it to help you decide on more important investment choices.

When should I do this spell?

Any time you are considering an investment venture

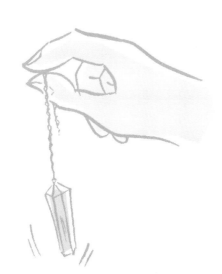

Holding Onto Your Money

What do I need?

One or more feng shui coins with a hole in the middle, or copper disks with a hole in the middle and with a sign on them denoting your currency, such as a dollar sign

A length of string or thin green ribbon for each room containing a tap or a toilet

A drawing pin for each room containing a tap or a toilet

The following spell combines Eastern and Western magical principles to help you keep hold of your money. In feng shui, money is related to the element of water, and feng shui practitioners correlate the state of your finances with the condition of the plumbing in your home or workplace. It is important to check that you have no leakages from your taps or pipes and that you keep the lid of your toilet and the door to the toilet closed when not in use.

What should I do?

First, go to each tap and check whether it is leaking and whether the sink needs a new plug. If needed, replace washers, buy new plugs and get your plumber in to check any persistent leaks.

Prepare each coin or copper disk by threading the string or ribbon through the hole in the center. Prepare as many coins as you have taps.

When you are ready, hang a coin or disk near each tap, securing the string or ribbon to the wall or other stable surface with a drawing pin. Make sure that the coin is well secured.

When should I do this spell?

On a Thursday

Protecting Your Good Fortune

What do I need?

A small amount of terra-cotta clay, or artificial clay that can be baked in the oven

A sharp-pointed knife

A length of leather thong

Once you have had a taste of good fortune, you may wish to do the following spell to help protect your good fortune. In addition, there is nothing better than sharing your good fortune with others, as this will spread and enhance the flow of good energy around you, providing you with more and more opportunities to tap into your own luck and that of others, and making room for more good fortune for yourself.

What should I do?

Shape your clay into a flat round disk and, using your knife, draw the following rune:

On the reverse of the disk, use the point of the knife to write your surname. Make a hole at the top of the disk so that your name and the rune hang right way up. Leave the terra-cotta to dry in the sun or bake the artificial clay in the oven, following the manufacturer's instructions. Hang the runic talisman over the door of your house or workplace.

The image of the rune stems from a protection rune called an algiz. This version of the protection rune symbolizes the strength and protection of the tree – in this spell it represents the taking root of good fortune, with the branches warding off any attempts to undermine your luck.

When should I do this spell?

On a Wednesday

What do I need?

A picture of the house or of the kind of house you want

A pair of scissors

A piece of paper

Glue

A black pen

A hole punch

A piece of string about 40 inches (100 cm) long

Home & Family

Attracting the Right House

One very important aspect of spellcraft is to know precisely what you want. Your mental clarity on this will often determine how successful your spell turns out to be. Take the time to hone your ideas about what you want, especially regarding major desires, such as having the right house. Start a scrapbook and fill it with pictures that have elements that you want in your home in terms of interior decoration and atmosphere.

What should I do?

Sit at a table to prepare this spell. Cut out a picture of the type of house you want. Paste it on a sheet of paper and cut off the excess paper.

On the back of the image, list important features of the house you want. Characteristics can range from physical features, such as the number of bedrooms, to the atmosphere and energy of your ideal home.

When should I do this spell?

Punch a hole near the bottom of the image and attach the string. Place the image as far away from you as the length of string allows. Relax and breathe deeply. Concentrate on the house you want, and start pulling the string so that the house moves slowly towards you.

On a Saturday

Keep pulling the string until the image of the house is under your hand. Pick up the picture and hang it in front of a window in your bedroom for three days and nights.

Finding the Right Place to Live

What do I need?

An amulet of protection, such as a jade bi. A jade bi is a round piece of jade with a hole in the middle.

Feng shui practitioners believe the ideal place to live is a place containing a harmonious flow of energy. It is important that the flow of energy meanders up to the front door, and that it is not obstructed within the house by awkwardly placed doors and furniture.

It is believed that a house that was the setting for a negative event, such as a divorce settlement or the former owners becoming bankrupt, should be avoided. It is also believed that a house should not be situated near a cemetery or church, or facing an oncoming road.

Even if you are not familiar with feng shui principles, you can still perceive whether the flow of energy in a house that you are inspecting is beneficial.

What should I do?

Walk to the front door or main entrance of the premises. Hang your amulet of protection around your neck or carry it in your pocket. Take three deep breaths and imagine that you can feel the energy flowing through the front door, and that you are caught up in the energy flow as you wander in and out of each room of the premises.

As you enter each room or area, feel or visualize the flow of energy moving in the room. If the energy feels slow or seems to disappear in a particular room or area, this is an indication of stagnant or poisoned energy that will require clearing if you choose this house.

Other indications of stagnant or poisonous energies include feeling a sharp chill upon first entering a room or the main hall of the house, the decay of interior features, dead plants in the garden, or a generally claustrophobic quality to the building.

For maximum success in your life, choose a house that does not exhibit such indications of stagnant energies.

When should I do this spell?

On a Saturday

Seeking Success for Your Children

What do I need?

A small crystal cluster that has one pointed crystal extending higher than the others. Chose clear or smoky quartz or an amethyst cluster.

Helping your children pass exams or be picked for the local sports team is often a matter of spending some time with them and lending a helping hand. To give them an extra edge, try the following spell.

What should I do?

Purchase the pointed crystal cluster that falls under your hand when you are in the shop and thinking of your child.

When you have brought the cluster home, blow any dust out of it, then rinse it carefully under running water. Pat the cluster dry, placing it on a stable surface where you can gaze upon it as you sit in a meditative state.

Sit comfortably and focus on your breathing, making sure it is even and steady. Concentrate on the pointed crystal that rises above the cluster. Imagine that this is symbolic of your child moving toward his or her true path and destiny.

Repeat the following words 33 times:

"May [insert name of child] succeed in [his or her] own true path."

Hold the crystal close to your heart and let all the love you feel for your child filter into the crystal. Place the crystal in your child's bedroom, making sure that it stays free from dust.

Never be tempted to force your child to succeed in a particular way or at a particular event. To do so may distract your child from his or her true path in the desire to please you.

When should I do this spell?

On a Wednesday

49

Attracting Success for Your Spouse's Ventures

What do I need?

A red pen

A piece of parchment or parchment-like paper big enough on which to write the name of your spouse or partner

An unopened small packet of dried mint leaves

A gold-colored envelope

A picture or photograph of a deer

Is your spouse or relationship partner starting up a new venture? Is he or she putting both heart and soul into the success of the business or other project? There is a way to honor such commitment by directing good wishes towards the fulfillment of their goals. Try the following spell as a supportive gesture.

What should I do?

Write your partner's name on the parchment or paper. On the reverse side of the paper, write the name of the business venture or the project. Slip

the parchment or paper and the unopened packet of dried mint leaves into the envelope and seal it. Write the talismanic letters shown on the next page on the front of the envelope and trace a triangle around them.

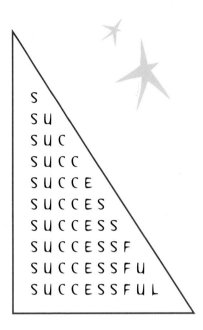

```
S
S U
S U C
S U C C
S U C C E
S U C C E S
S U C C E S S
S U C C E S S F
S U C C E S S F U
S U C C E S S F U L
```

When should
I do this
spell?

On a Wednesday

The triangle is believed to be a powerful symbol of wisdom.

Paste your picture of a deer onto the back of the envelope. The deer is a Chinese symbol of longevity and good financial success. Place this envelope on the mantelpiece or on the top shelf of a bookcase in the main living area.

Harmony Spell

ncouraging harmony between family members can be challenging. However, the following spell will clear out negative stagnant energy created by bickering and the occasional screaming match or door banging session. Once this kind of energy is cleared from your home, there is room to attract a more harmonious atmosphere.

What should I do?

Constant arguments make the air of an area feel heavy, sound flat or seem dull in color (as if the area is covered in a light layer of dust). When you detect such an area in your home, ring the bell over the space, particularly over upholstered pieces of furniture, which soak up a lot of energy through close contact with people. Keep ringing until you sense a change in the air.

If the whole house has resonated from family arguments, walk through the house, starting from the front door. Ring a bell at every doorway and check that none of your doors stick or jam. If they do, get a carpenter to work on the doors as soon as possible, so that they no longer stick. Sticking or creaking doors indicate a poor flow of energy through the house.

Once you have finished, sit in the area where the last argument was waged. Run through the situation that led to the argument and visualize a different ending in which resolution was achieved. Imagine a successful outcome after a respectful negotiation.

Burn the stick of lavender incense to anchor a calmer energy into the area and to honor the visualization that you have just done. You may also wish to walk through the house with the incense stick to carry the blessing of calmness and harmony into every area of your home.

When should I do this spell?

During the phase of the new moon or on a Monday

Spells When Things Go Wrong

* ★ ☆ *

Getting Back on Track

What do I need?

A sapphire (preferably uncut, making it a cheaper option) or a turquoise

The Hermit card from your favorite Tarot deck

A piece of paper

Your favorite pen

A blue bag big enough to carry the stone and paper

It sometimes happens that you lose your drive to succeed. Often this is caused by an inner realization that maybe you were trying to succeed at something that was not really your true calling, or that would not have led you to, or helped you along, your true path. Getting back on track can often require a time of self-assessment, and a search for a path through life which is truly your own. This spell will help you work out your true path. It is important to know that there is no such thing as failure; there is merely delay.

What should I do?

Hold the sapphire or turquoise in your left hand if you are right-handed, or in your right hand if you are left-handed. Sapphires are believed to encourage truthfulness, and wearing or holding one will help

54

you keep to your true path. Turquoise is often used as a protection against misfortune. Be conscious of your breathing – breathe in and out deeply and steadily.

Focus on the Hermit card, feeling yourself going more deeply into a meditative state. This card represents the willingness of a person to withdraw and meditate on things that have gone wrong, and accesses your inherent ability to find new wisdom with which to move on successfully with your life.

While meditating on this card, write down any ideas or suggestions that spring to mind. It is important at this stage not to analyze these thoughts. Jot them down quickly and concisely on the piece of paper. When you feel ready, close your eyes and have a rest.

Quickly fold the paper and pop it into the bag along with the sapphire or turquoise. Carry this bag with you until the next new moon. You will find that your true path will become clearer or the way to get back on track will already be forming.

When should I do this spell?

During the phase of the new moon

Loss of Money

What do I need?

A piece of cardboard the size of a business card

Some marker pens of different colors

There are many spells to protect against loss of money, but few for coping when money has already been lost. Try the following spell to help you stop any further loss of money and to encourage a sense of internal fortitude. Two powerful symbols will be combined for this spell – the eye, as protection against the evil eye, and the fish, symbolic of fortitude and abundance. The fish also represents going with the flow, finding the right stream to reach the sea of plenty.

What should I do?

The spell involves making a special talisman that will help to stop the further loss of money. The talisman is a combination of symbols drawn onto the business-card-sized piece of cardboard.

Draw a rowing boat (do not bother with the oars). On the front end or prow of the boat, draw a simple version of a fish. Within the body of the fish, draw a circle with a dot in the middle. Use as many colours to draw this picture as you like.

This is called a fish eye. It combines the mystical properties of the eye, which serves as a protection against the evil eye and is also symbolic of a spiritual guardian, and the fish, which represents fertility and fortitude concerning the increase of wealth. This amulet will help you withstand your loss and get back onto your feet financially.

Tidy out your wallet or purse and clean it with a soft cloth. Tuck the amulet into your wallet or purse, and keep an "eye out" for new financial opportunities and financial wisdom.

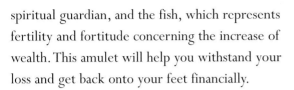

When should I do this spell?

On a Thursday

Getting a New Job

What do I need?

A symbol of your old work, such as paperwork or one of your smaller tools

A shallow box without a lid into which all the ingredients in this list will fit

A bunch of rosemary

A symbol of the new work you wish to attract, for example, an ad cut out of the newspaper

If you have been fired or have lost your job because the company went bankrupt, setting about the process of getting a new job may feel depressing. You will often need to cleanse yourself of the bad experience before you are ready to move on.

The following spell exorcises the negative feelings connected with losing your old job, while allowing you to learn any important lessons that you need to have learned from the experience before attracting an even better job.

What should I do?

Bring home some old paperwork or a tool that can be used as a symbol of your old work (do not use anything that you are not entitled to remove from the office). Place this symbol at the bottom of your box and cover it with the bunch of rosemary. The rosemary acts as a cleanser of old, hurtful memories.

Next, place on top of the rosemary a symbol of the type of work you are seeking. If your symbol is a job advertisement, paste the advertisement onto the paper and staple the tassel over the ad. The red tassel is a feng shui symbol attracting good fortune and abundance.

If there is no job description for what you want to do, simply write the name of your desired position on the piece of paper, and staple the red tassel over the word.

Place the box, without a lid, on top of the tallest piece of furniture you own – for example, the wardrobe or a high bookshelf – for three days and nights. Watch out for new opportunities becoming available to you. For a spell concerning success at a job interview, see pages 24–25.

also ...

A sheet of A4 paper

Glue

A stapler and staples

A small red tassel

When should I do this spell?

On a Wednesday

Loss of Respect

What do I need?

A sheet of paper

A pair of scissors

A silver bowl of water

A piece of polished moonstone

A small white bag

*L*oss of respect and credibility is painful. The following spell will let you face the truth of your predicament, why you acted in the way you did, and help you tap into your inherent sense of integrity to help turn the situation around. The spell will also help you work out the right thing to do – perhaps an apology is required, or you need to make an attempt to set things right.

What should I do?

Sit outside or near a window where you can see the moon. Cut the paper into six pieces. Position the silver bowl of water so that the image of the moon is captured in the water. Hold the moonstone while contemplating the moon's image in the water.

The moon is symbolic of intuition and sanity as well as confusion and unbalanced thinking. By contemplating the moon when you have lost respect through some form of irresponsible action or error, you are linking into its dark aspects. However, it is also symbolic of light, encouraging your intuition to help you right the situation.

As you focus on the moon, ask it a question, such as:

"How may I rectify this situation?"

Using one segment of paper for each thought, jot down any thoughts that come to mind. Write the thoughts down quickly and do not analyze them for their viability. Next, fold each piece of paper in half.

When you feel ready, throw the pieces of paper into the bowl of water. Some will sink, while others will float momentarily on the surface of the water. The first suggestion that floats close to the image of the moon is the most viable suggestion.

Put the suggestion and the moonstone together in the small white bag. Carry it with you for three days and nights to anchor the suggestion to your reality.

When should I do this spell?

During the phase of the full moon

61

Making Things Right

What do I need?

A piece of parchment or a sheet of parchment-like paper

Your favorite blue pen

A small box, preferably made of pine

The dried petals of a pink carnation

A piece of hematite

When you are in the unfortunate position of having caused someone hurt or harm in an attempt to obtain success, you must right the situation by undoing some of the damage that was inflicted. The harm you have caused others may be stopping you from obtaining the success you desire.

The following healing spell will help you commit to unselfishly helping the person whom you have harmed. There may be a number of ways you can help, and you will need to think of what is suitable for your particular circumstance. However, by choosing this solution, you will be able to overcome feelings of guilt or shame, and will ultimately be able to attract further success in your life.

What should I do?

On the top of the piece of paper, write the name of the person you have harmed. On the next line, write down how that person was hurt. On the next several lines, write down all the things you commit to do for that person.

Fold the sheet of paper and place it into the wooden box, along with the pink carnation petals and the hematite. Close the lid and place the spell box near your telephone or fax machine, or in another area in your home where a lot of communication occurs.

The pine box, the carnation and the hematite are excellent symbols of healing, as is the blue ink of your pen. A pink carnation is used because pink represents compassion and friendship.

For the spell to work properly, you must actually do the things you have committed to doing. If you don't, you may find yourself in a worse state than the one you were in to begin with.

When should I do this spell?

On a Sunday

Protecting Against Envy

What do I need?

A handful of sea salt

A bowl of water

A picture of the envious person

A red ribbon

A hand mirror with a handle made of pine or cedar

An effective way of countering envy, and gossip born of envy or jealousy, is to refocus the envious person's attention on him or herself. This can be done through mirror magic. The following spell works well if you can identify the person who is feeling envious or jealous.

What should I do?

Throw some of the salt into the bowl of water. Collect the other ingredients of the spell (including the rest of the sea salt) and sprinkle the salted water in a circle enclosing you and your spell materials.

Place the picture of the envious person face up on a stable surface. Tie the red ribbon around the handle of the mirror and place it face down on top of the picture. This symbolizes the neutralizing of

the person's envious comments. The salted water and the red ribbon represent protection.

Sprinkle the remaining sea salt over the back of the hand mirror, leaving the ingredients arranged in this way overnight.

When should I do this spell?

During the phase of the full moon

What do I need?

A moonstone

A piece of cardboard about the size of a business card

A green pen

Four lavender spikes

A purple bag big enough to accommodate all ingredients

Good Luck Spells

All-Purpose Good Luck Spell

Attracting good luck is another area in which many traditional spells have developed, taking the form of a written word, a symbol that can be worn around the neck, or a combination of ingredients that can be worn or imbibed. The spell below combines a number of traditional ingredients into a super-spell of good luck.

What should I do?

Bathe the moonstone in the light of the new moon by holding up the stone so that it covers or partially covers the moon. Take three deep breaths and visualize the moon's rays caressing the stone and imbuing it with lucky qualities.

In the middle of the cardboard, draw the outline of a four-leaf clover, using your green pen. Within one leaf write, in small letters, the word "Fame"; in the second leaf write "Faithful Lover"; in the third leaf write "Good Health"; and in the fourth leaf write "Wealth."

When should I do this spell?

During the phase of the new moon

Around the four-leaf clover draw a circle, which is the simplest and most powerful symbol of protection. Around the circle write your full name, repeating the name as often as it takes to complete the circle.

Put the moonstone, the business card and the lavender into the bag. Make sure that the bag is made from natural materials, such as silk, cotton, linen, flax, hemp or leather.

This bag can be combined with other images to attract good luck for specific projects and wishes. To direct the good luck energy to a particular desire, store the good luck bag for three days and nights with a symbol of what you want. For example, if you want a new house or car, store the bag with an image of a house or car or some object that symbolizes your wish.

Finding a Good Luck Amulet

What do I need?

Comfortable walking shoes

A cotton handkerchief to keep the found object safe

Many types of good luck amulets exist. Often, the most powerful are the ones you find in the garden or when walking along a tree-lined street, that give you a sense of receiving a special gift from nature.

What should I do?

Set apart a time to take a walk dedicated toward finding a good luck amulet. Take the handkerchief with you on the walk. To dedicate the walk to this purpose, simply say the following words before you leave your home through the front door:

"I will find a good luck charm that will help me obtain the luck I deserve."

Go for your walk. Ideally, do not plan your walk, apart from heading off to leafy areas, such as parks. As you walk, feel that you are sending out signals that you are seeking a good luck charm. Be aware of where you step and take note of what catches your eye.

Your path may lead you across a discarded, half-buried horseshoe, a beautiful feather from your favorite bird, or a beautiful piece of bark that has fallen from a tree. Keep a watchful eye for an object that resonates with feelings of good luck for you.

When you find the right object, pick it up and wrap it up in your cotton handkerchief. Carry it back home with you. Place the object, still wrapped up, under your pillow for three nights. This will anchor the amulet's connection with you.

When should I do this spell?

During the phase of a new moon

Making a
Good Luck Charm

What do I need?

A branch or stick fallen from an old oak tree

A white linen cloth, large enough in which to wrap the branch

A white-handled knife

A black marker pen

Salted water

A candle in a candle holder

A stick of incense

A handful of dirt

charm is a spell in which a word or verse is written on parchment, paper or an object to attract good luck. You will need a powerful word, something to write it on and something to contain the magic of the written charm. The word does not have to be in English. Since ancient times, runes have been used to attract magic. Using runic symbols in conjunction with wood will enhance the power of the ancient charm.

What should I do?

Identify the oak trees in your neighborhood, and check them after particularly windy days to see whether any branches or sticks have blown to the ground. When you find one, keep it wrapped in a white linen cloth until the phase of the new moon.

When you are ready, take the wood and, with the knife, cut it down to a manageable size. Then whittle down a flat surface upon which you can carve or simply write the rune on the following page.

70

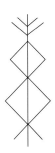

This rune is a combination of runic symbols, and is called a bind rune. With this rune, the good luck you will attract will take the form of prosperity and well-being.

During the phase of the new moon

To enhance the power of your lucky charm, consecrate it to your desire by invoking the four elements. To consecrate means to dedicate the object to your desire. You can do this by sprinkling the charm with salted water (water), passing it quickly over the flame of a candle (fire), passing it through the smoke of incense (air), and then sprinkling earth over it (earth).

71

Good Luck in Games of Chance

What do I need?

A key

A piece of carnelian

A gold or silver silk bag

If you occasionally dabble in playing games of chance, you probably already have your own rituals to help improve your chances. You may have a favorite ring that you always wear to bring you luck, or you may always bet on a particular number because you feel that it is your lucky number.

There are many traditions concerning how to attract "Lady Luck" to you. As she is known to be fickle, you need to rely on your instincts about how long to play a game, when to move on to another game, and when to simply go home.

If you feel obsessed about the next turn of the card, this is a very clear indication that you have lost access to your instincts. Go home immediately. The best time to gamble is when you feel detached and can sense the flow of energy around the room or track.

Try the following spell to help you keep in touch with your instincts.

What should I do?

Hold the key in your right hand if you are right-handed, or in your left hand if you are left-handed. This is going to represent the key to your instincts if you get into a rut when gambling.

Visualize this key opening a door where you see yourself winning a game without seeming to try or care. Touching this key will help you move away from any potentially destructive behavior. It will also help you focus properly again.

Place the key and the carnelian into the silk bag. The carnelian will help encourage the voice of your intuition to assert itself when you are feeling a bit too mesmerized by the game.

When should I do this spell?

On a Wednesday

Success for a Risky Venture

What do I need?

A piece of green-colored aventurine

Access to running water, preferably in natural surroundings

A white linen or cotton handkerchief

A handful of earth or sand from the beach or bank next to the running water

A small bottle or jar

Three drops of frankincense essential oil

isky ventures have inspired the creation of spells since time immemorial, most of them designed to help bring to fruition a dream or hope, or to help a project survive. The following spell blends some time-honored traditions that combine the elements and help realign the energies around you for success.

What should I do?

At any time, wash the aventurine in a running brook, a creek or in the ocean. Wipe it with the handkerchief and let both the stone and the cloth dry naturally. Take some of the water and some of the earth or sand from the beach or riverbed home in a bottle or jar.

On a Wednesday, collect all the ingredients of the spell and arrange them on a stable surface. Measure out three drops of the essential oil directly onto the candle and rub the oil into the candle's surface. This is called anointing the candle. With the white-handled knife, carve the word "Success" down the side of the candle.

Light the incense and the candle. Place the candle in a stable and fire-proof candle holder. Pour the water into the chalice, keeping the dregs of the earth or sand at the bottom of the bottle or jar.

Hold the aventurine in your hand and imagine the project you are working on becoming a success. When you feel ready, place the stone in the middle of the dry handkerchief and pass it over the candle flame, the incense smoke, the water and the earth.

Now, tie a knot in each corner of the handkerchief, placing the aventurine in the center of it. Collect the edges of the handkerchief so that it is covering the stone, and tie the green ribbon so as to secure the stone within the folds of the cloth. Place the parcel near the black candle, and let the candle burn out overnight. Make sure that the candle cannot splutter and set fire to the bundle.

Carry the stone and handkerchief with you to important meetings or other events that have a bearing on the outcome of the project.

also ...

A black candle

A white-handled knife

Matches

A stick of frankincense incense

A candle holder

A chalice

A length of green ribbon

𝒲𝒽𝑒𝓃 𝓈𝒽𝑜𝓊𝓁𝒹 𝒥 𝒹𝑜 𝓉𝒽𝒾𝓈 𝓈𝓅𝑒𝓁𝓁?

On a Wednesday

75

Getting Accepted

What do I need?

A sturdy piece of cardboard about 4 inches (10 cm) square

Your favorite pen

A purple bag big enough to contain the ingredients of the spell

Eight unshelled hazelnuts

Eight coffee beans in a small plastic bag

A small piece of amethyst

etting accepted into a project, course, or even a group with which you'd like to be involved, may require eloquence and persuasiveness. To enhance these skills, you may wish to invoke the help of the energy that resonates with the planet Mercury. The following spell gives instructions on how to make a Mercury talisman.

What should I do?

On the cardboard, draw the grid shown below, with its 64 numbers. Make sure the numbers are in the correct place.

8	58	59	5	4	62	63	1
49	15	14	52	53	11	10	56
41	23	22	44	48	19	18	45
32	34	38	29	25	35	39	28
40	26	27	37	36	30	31	33
17	47	46	20	21	43	42	24
9	55	51	12	13	54	50	16
64	2	3	61	60	6	7	57

When you are finished, place the cardboard into your bag with the hazelnuts, the coffee beans and the amethyst. Eight coffee beans and eight hazelnuts are used because each row of this magic square adds up to 260 (2 + 6 + 0 = 8). Place the bag near you when you are specifically working towards getting accepted.

If your wish involves the signing of a contract or other document – for example, because you have won the tender or a publisher has accepted your novel – sign the document with the pen you used in this spell.

When should I do this spell?

On a Wednesday

Glossary

Amulet — a protective device worn around the neck or hung from the door or window of a sacred space or home.

Chalice — or cup, one of the elemental tools symbolizing water and the emotions.

Charm — a magical word or words that can be used for protection.

Circle — a sacred space, usually thought of as a sphere of energy created when the circle is cast.

Consecrate — to make a small dedication of your spell to a particular purpose.

Elements — it is believed in Western magic that four elements make up the physical world, including our bodies — earth, air, fire and water.

Feng shui — a traditional Chinese system of balance, placement and design based on understanding the flow of energy in the world and the cosmos.

Grounding – connecting the body's energy with that of the earth.

Invoke – to summon a spirit or energy form into oneself.

Runes – magical symbols first used by ancient Nordic and Germanic cultures. These symbols can be used for divination (seeking the future and understanding the past) and are inscribed on talismans and amulets.

Tarot – a deck of cards used as a form of divination. The deck comprises 78 cards, which are divided into the major arcana of 22 cards and the minor arcana of 56 cards. The minor arcana are further divided into four groups, representing the four elements.

Talisman – an object charged to attract a specific magical energy.

This edition published by Barnes & Noble, Inc.,
by arrangement with Lansdowne Publishing

2001 Barnes & Noble Books

M 10 9 8 7 6 5 4 3 2 1

ISBN 0-7607-2743-0

Published by Lansdowne Publishing Pty Ltd
Sydney NSW 2000, Australia

Commissioned by Deborah Nixon
Text: Antonia Beattie
Illustrated by: Sue Rawkins, Sue Ninham, Joanna Davies, Jane Cameron,
Penny Lovelock
Cover art: Sue Ninham
Designer: Sue Rawkins
Editor: Sarah Shrubb
Production Manager: Sally Stokes
Project Co-ordinator: Kylie Lowson

Set in Perpetua and Gigi on QuarkXPress
Printed in China, produced by Jade Productions